MONKEYS

Chimpanzees

Mae Woods
ABDO & Daughters

visit us at
www.abdopub.com

Published by Abdo & Daughters, 4940 Viking Drive, Suite 622, Edina, Minnesota 55435.

Copyright © 1998 by Abdo Consulting Group, Inc., Pentagon Tower, P.O. Box 36036, Minneapolis, Minnesota 55435 USA. International copyrights reserved in all countries. No part of this book may be reproduced in any form without written permission from the publisher.

Printed in the United States.

Cover Photo credits: Peter Arnold, Inc.
Interior Photo credits: Peter Arnold, Inc.

Edited by Lori Kinstad Pupeza

Library of Congress Cataloging-in-Publication Data

Woods, Mae.
        Chimpanzees / Mae Woods.
                p.   cm. -- (Monkeys)
        Includes index.
        Summary: Describes the physical characteristics, habitat, habits, and
        behavior of the much-studied members of the Great Ape family.
        ISBN 1-56239-597-1
        1. Chimpanzees--Juvenile literature. [1. Chimpanzees.] I. Title. II. Series:
        Woods, Mae. Monkeys.
        QL737.P96W64 1998
        599.88'44--dc20   96-11384
                                                                 CIP
                                                                 AC

Contents

Chimpanzees and Other Primates

In earlier times, the African name for the chimpanzee was "the mockman." These clever apes are a lot like humans and they have the ability to **mimic** or **mock** what they see.

The chimpanzee is part of the family of Great Apes, which also includes **gorillas** and **orangutans**. Apes, humans, and monkeys are all **primates**. Humans have the largest brain, but the chimpanzee uses **intelligence** to think the same way people do.

Chimpanzees learn quickly. They can be easily trained because they have good memories. They are also good at problem solving. They can learn **sign language** and use it to **communicate** with humans.

Over the years, scientists have done many

studies with these animals because they are so much like humans. In 1961, a trained chimp named Ham was dressed in a pressure suit and sent into space in a rocket. The **mission** was successful and made it possible for astronauts to travel to the moon.

Chimps grooming each other.

Where They Live

Chimpanzees live in many **regions** of central, eastern, and western Africa. Many make their homes in the tropical rain forests, but some live on the flat, open grasslands.

When they can, chimpanzees prefer living on the edges of forests. When they settle there, they can search for food on the plains during the day and still go back home to sleep in the trees where they will be safe from other animals when it is dark.

In one forest area in Central Africa there is an ape that looks very much like a chimpanzee. Though it has many of the same **features**, scientists now call it the **bonobo**. It is very rare.

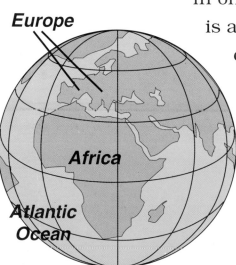

Europe

Africa

Atlantic Ocean

6

A chimp hanging from a tree limb in Tanzania, Africa.

What They Are Like

The face of a chimpanzee looks like an **orangutan**. Chimpanzees have small, flat noses and golden brown eyes with ridged brows. They have large mouths and can move their lips into a smile, a frown, or even a pucker for a kiss. Their large ears are on the sides of their heads and look like human ears.

The chimpanzees' skin color varies from light brown to black. Their bodies are covered with long black hair. The face and hands of a chimpanzee are hairless.

Chimpanzees are tail-less like all apes. But unlike the other apes, a chimpanzee's arms and legs are equal in length. All the other apes have arms that are longer and stronger than their legs. Chimpanzees are able to swing through the trees like orangutans and **gibbons**, but their arms soon tire. If they have far to travel, they walk on the ground instead. Chimpanzees usually travel in a "knuckle walk" like **gorillas**. They are able to stand and walk upright, but their knees are always slightly bent.

Chimpanzees weigh about 120 pounds and stand 4 feet tall. The male is only slightly larger than the female. Chimpanzees are fully grown at age 13. They can live to age 50. Like humans, their hair turns gray as they age. They may even become bald.

Chimpanzees use their arms to help them walk.

Groups

Chimpanzees live in groups. A group may be as large as 80 animals. Chimpanzees spend most of their day in the trees, and they sleep there at night. They build nests by weaving branches together and covering them with a bed of leaves and twigs.

These animals are more **independent** than the other apes and monkeys that live in troops. Chimpanzees like to roam about on their own or with a few friends. Often mothers and babies travel by themselves.

After a group settles in one area, the animals guard their **borders** to keep out other chimpanzee groups. If outsiders do appear, the chimpanzees will strike a **fierce** pose with their hair standing on end. They charge and scream and throw sticks. This usually scares away the other animals.

Chimpanzees spend most of their days in the trees.

Group Leader

Each group has a male leader who receives special treatment. The chimpanzees will actually bend and present their backs to their leader in a kind of reverse bow when they meet. This is called **presenting**.

The leader takes the best food. All the animals stay out of his way. Males may try to become the new leader by challenging him. Sometimes, the animal that shouts the loudest and looks the most **fierce** gets to be the leader. Chimpanzees do not like to fight with each other.

Opposite page: A male chimpanzee resting.

Food

Chimpanzees eat fruit, plants, leaves, bark, roots, vegetables, bird eggs, and insects. They do not eat much meat.

They are very smart. They make tools to use for eating food. A chimpanzee will put a stick into an insect colony and wait until the insects climb up the stick. Then the chimpanzee will pull it out and gobble them up. Chimpanzees use stones to crack open nuts. They also use leaves to scoop up water to drink.

These apes have learned about the plants around them. They will eat certain bitter leaves for **medicine** if they have a stomach ache. They know that the tough **stalks** of some plants have soft, juicy insides. They will suck out the sweet **pith** and spit out all the rough **fibers**.

Figs are the chimpanzees favorite food. When these fruits ripen, the group celebrates. The animals hoot loudly and drum on the fig trees to alert the rest of the group. Chimpanzees have a good sense of **rhythm**. They shout and pound their hands and feet in a kind of dance. Then they all feast on the figs.

A chimpanzee feeding on berries.

Babies

A newborn chimpanzee stays very close to its mother. It drinks her milk and nestles in her lap for warmth and comfort. When the mother chimpanzee goes into the trees to feed, the infant rides along holding onto the hair on her stomach. Once it is strong enough to climb onto her back, the baby will ride along on top of her as she travels.

When it is five months old, the baby will be able to stand. Soon it will begin to climb trees. The little chimp wants to explore everything it sees, but it never goes far from its mother's side. It sleeps in her nest at night.

Opposite page: A chimp grooming its baby.

Growing Up

The mother **grooms** the little one each day. She smooths out the tangles in the baby's hair and picks out any dirt or twigs. All chimpanzees enjoy being groomed. As the baby grows, it will take turns grooming its mother and its playmates. This is a way of showing friendship.

From childhood on, chimpanzees are very **affectionate**. They hug and kiss and pat each other on the back. They like to play together. They tickle each other, roll on the ground, and wrestle. They play tug-of-war with sticks. Young chimpanzees sometimes even play with baby baboons.

Opposite page: A mother chimp carrying her young.

Friends

Chimpanzees often have a close best friend. These two are very loving. They hold hands, cuddle, and kiss. They take turns **grooming** each other.

There are at least 34 different chimpanzee sounds. Every animal knows the meaning of each different call. They hoot when they find food. They scream to show fear or rage. A loud bark is a threat.

Chimpanzees also make many gestures and facial expressions. When chimpanzees grin and show their teeth, that is a threat. When they open their mouth with the upper teeth hidden, they are being friendly. A pouty mouth means they are thinking.

When chimpanzees are excited, they want to share their feelings with their friends. They hold hands when they are scared. They hug when they greet each other. If they have been apart for a long time, they will whoop and throw their arms around each other to show how happy they are to be together again.

Male chimps grooming each other.

Glossary

affectionate - Loving.

bonobo - An ape that was once called a pygmy chimpanzee.

border - The place where one area ends and another begins.

communicate (kuh-mew-nih-KATE) - To express thoughts and ideas.

features (FEH-cherz) - Parts of the face; special parts.

fibers - The threads that form the parts of plants that cannot be digested.

fierce (firs) - Savage or cruel.

gibbon (GIB-uhn) - A small, long-armed ape found in Southeast Asia and the East Indies.

gorilla (guh-RIL-uh) - The largest of the Great Apes.

groom - To clean and care for.

independent - Being in charge of oneself; thinking as an individual.

intelligence (in-TEL-ijens) - The ability to learn and understand or to solve problems.

medicine (MED i sin) - A substance used to take away pain or heal sickness.

mimic (MIM-ik) - To imitate.

mission (MISH-en) - A special duty or job.

mock (MAHK) - To make fun of or mimic.

orangutan (uh-RANG-uh-tan) - A red-haired Great Ape found in Southeast Asia.

patrol (pah-TROL) - To make regular trips.

pith - The soft, spongy tissue in the center of plant stems.

presenting - The apes gesture of bowing to a leader.

primates (PRIE-maytz) - A group of animals that include humans, apes, and monkeys.

regions (RE-jens) - Areas.

rhythm (rith-ehm) - The form or movement of sound with beats coming at certain times.

sign language - A system of hand gestures used to express ideas.

species (SPEE-sheez) - A group of animals that are alike in certain ways.

stalks (stawkz) - The stems of a plant.

Index